THE
HEART OF HEALING

A JOURNAL OF
REMARKABLE DEMONSTRATIONS
OF GOD'S HEALING POWER
(1927)

Mizanna Wolff

ISBN 0-7661-0373-0

The Heart of Healing

A Journal of Remarkable Demonstrations of God's Healing Power

By MIZANNA WOLFF

L. N. Fowler & Co.
Ludgate Circus, London

———

Published by
THE ELIZABETH TOWNE CO., INC.
HOLYOKE, MASS.

Printed in U.S.A.

CONTENTS

CHAPTER 1

How To Apply The Truth That Frees From Sorrow, Sickness And Pain

WHEN Jesus said, "Come unto me all ye that labor and are heavy laden and I will give you rest," he was not speaking to only a chosen few but he meant just what he said—"*ALL.*" And not until we come into the full realization of this wonderful invitation, can we fully appreciate what a blessed privilege it is to be invited to come to the Father, under all conditions. Sickness, sorrow and pain, will vanish as if by magic when we accept this standing invitation. There is no problem too big or too complicated, to be taken care of when we go to The Father with it. I believe if we spent half as much time in Communion with God as we spend in idle gossip, we would never have pain, sorrow or poverty. I wish I could prevail upon every one to set aside *just 15 minutes* three times a day, for the silence where one can get in touch with the divine Wisdom within, and there find rest.

It is a very difficult proposition to make a set of rules for the mass of people and expect them to work satisfactorily in every case, for no two persons receive the same impressions or interpretations. Just as no two thumb prints are exactly alike, so do we each receive our very own impressions, each one different from all others. But on the whole, all that is necessary, is to seek God in his secret place and hold this statement:

> Father, thou art the God of love, wisdom and power and with thee all things are possible. Sorrow, sickness and strife vanish in thy presence. I thank thee that all is well in every department of life. I am at peace with myself and with all the world.

I realize that it is difficult, for the beginner in Truth to grasp and hold tight to a Truth statement, at first, for as a rule most of us have been hampered to some degree by family teachings, but we can come into the realization of these statements by persistence, patience, and practice. What I mean by this is to constantly affirm the TRUTH STATE-MENT and realize that "I AND THE FATHER ARE ONE." Then ask for what you want, believing you will receive it, then prepare to receive it and you will receive it, providing it doesn't harm any one or anything.

Now do not become discouraged just because you are slow to demonstrate, because, dear reader, the babe must first learn to crawl before it can walk and it must walk before it can run. If one makes successful demonstrations in Truth too early, he is apt to become egotistical and careless and prone to misconstrue their real value and thereby retard his real spiritual growth in the Truth.

Never try to demonstrate anything that you cannot say is in DIVINE HARMONY with the all good. If you ask in the right kind of spirit you will never have cause for doubt or disappointment. (At least I never do). Ask and believe, praise and be thankful, even though you didn't get just exactly what you wanted. Remember that practice makes perfect.

"I WILL NEVER LEAVE THEE NOR FORSAKE THEE." Heb. 13:5.

CHAPTER II

How God Restored The Use Of My Arms After Several Doctors Had Failed

SOME years ago, before I had demonstrated much, I had the misfortune to be thrown from a street car, injuring the spine. The result was complete paralysis, or complete loss of the power of motion.

For seven months I had to be taken care of just like a six-month-old-baby. I couldn't move either my arms or limbs. Of course we had several doctors, to be exact we had four; but none of them seemed to be able to give me any relief, so we discarded all but one and he came daily for several months. Still I did not get any better. The doctor finally told the family that one arm would never get any better. But he said I might possibly be able to use the other one after a while. I suffered constantly, despite everything.

One day, after a very bad week and when every one around me was in despair, a dear old lady asked to be allowed to pray for me. She prayed such a wonderful prayer that I immediately felt better, and I asked her to come again the next day, which she gladly did. She came every day after that and with each visit I improved, until at the end of one month I could move myself quite a bit, slide my feet on the floor, and feed myself, and I was completely out of pain. I refused to have the physician after the first prayer, for *I knew that GOD was doing the HEALING work.*

I kept up the statement that the dear old lady had taught me. I use it yet sometimes, and I have taught it to several others, and it has always helped all who have used it. The statement:

> I am a child of God. His
> love flows through me and fills
> me with love, life and liberty.
> I am every whit whole. I am
> perfect as my Father in heaven
> would have me to be.

I do not intend to weary you with many healing experiences but only give a few to prove to you that God's Law, when rightly used, is sufficient for all our needs and when we live with this Law predominating in our lives, we will always be at our best.

CHAPTER III

Preparing To Receive Your Desire

WHEN you are told to hold a statement, or a thought, that doesn't mean that you have done your part toward receiving your desire, for you have not. True, you have started the thing you desire coming your way; but you must do more than ask and sit down. You must also make plans to receive your desire by opening up every channel that it is possible for you to do. Picture yourself in possession of the thing sought for, be happy in the thought that you have it, then thank God for it.

I have demonstrated so many things that I could not tell you of all of them. I demonstrate something every day, for life seems to demand so much. But I always try to put into life as much as I draw out. Thus, when I receive a blessing I try to make someone, or something, happy in turn. I find that the more we put into life the more we get out of life.

Once I wrote a story and I asked the Father to help me sell it. I sent that story out to the editor of a magazine, accompanied by God's blessing. I then sat down and spoke this editor's name and told him that he had received a story from me. Here I spoke aloud the title of my story. I told the editor that it was a splendid story. I called his attention to its merits, its high lights, its humor and its pathos. I then visualized the editor reading it. I saw him write a check, I saw the amount called for was $25. I saw our banker giving me the money in one ten and three five dollar bills.

And it all happened just that way, in exactly 15 days after I sent out my story. I thanked God for my check and asked him to bless that editor. And I always ask God's blessing to rest upon all the people who do anything for me. That is, I ask for a *special* blessing for them.

"WHAT THINGS SOEVER YE DESIRE, WHEN YE PRAY, BELIEVE THAT YE RECEIVE THEM, AND YE SHALL HAVE THEM." Mark 11:24.

CHAPTER IV

How God's Love Helped Me Overcome Old Age And Sickness

MY EARLY life, until I accepted God's Love, was spent in sickness and sorrow. At the age of 28 years I was what would be termed a middle-aged woman. I was thin, pale and weak. No one thought I would ever be robust and most people thought I would never live to be thirty.

All my life I had been under some doctor's care. I seemed to have almost everything that the human family is liable to and a few other things that were not in the medical books or known to the profession. The list included tuberculosis. Life meant nothing to me. Everything was dark, not one ray of light did the future hold forth to me. I was so discouraged that I didn't have any desire to keep on living. Returning from a visit to my physician one morning, I had the misfortune to be thrown from the car in such a manner that I received an injury that left me a helpless invalid. I was so helpless that I needed constant

14

care. The physicians said nothing could be done for me. But a friend prayed to God to heal me, and he did. I then began to practice New Thought statements and to live New Thought. And now, at the age of 42, I am robust, well and happy, and I look at least ten years younger than I did fourteen years ago.

I am well from head to foot, without an ache or pain, THANKS TO GOD.

After so many years of sickness my hair began to turn grey and was very thin. I used this statement on it and now I have a heavy thatch of black hair, long and curly. For those were the things I asked for and they are what I received. The statement follows:

Hair, you are beautiful. You are black, lustrous, long, thick and curly. You are the glory that my Father in heaven gave to me and I thank him.

"ALL THINGS ARE POSSIBLE TO HIM THAT BELIEVETH." Mark 9:23.

CHAPTER V

How Love Collected A Debt Of Eleven Years' Standing, With Interest

WHILE keeping a nursery in Kansas City, a gentleman brought me a three-months-old baby to care for. Its mother had deserted both the baby and its father. I was to give it food, lodging, care and laundry for $30. a month.

At first the man came to see the baby once a week and paid the bill regularly. Then gradually he stopped coming so often, but he kept the bill paid up for a year. He then told me he was planning to get married again, and he would then take the baby. But he began to fall behind with her board, until when he came to take her home he was $60. in arrears. He gave me a good excuse why he couldn't pay the bill. Of course, I could have demanded my money, but someway I felt sorry for him and I loved the baby, so I told him it was all right, he could pay me when it suited him best. Well, he moved away from the city and I didn't hear from him for over nine years. Then I saw an item in the paper where he had come into an estate, and that he was coming back to the city to enter the business firm of his father. I waited another two years, and as he had not paid me and I felt that I had given good service for this money, and that it was mine by Divine right, I took the matter into the silence thus:

> I thank thee, my Father that I have only good will toward Mr.——————— and I thank thee because he bears only good will toward me and I thank thee for the payment of the money that he owes to me.

I did not wish to acknowledge that he *still* owed me, so I put it in that way so it would be all the stronger in my favor, for I wanted my treatment to be a success. Here I stopped and mentally counted out the money. I counted it out in *silver dollars* because it seemed so much bigger. Then I thought, as I had waited 11 years for the money I surely was entitled to some interest, so I counted out *two more dollars* for myself. Then I asked that GOD'S BLESSING ABIDE WITH THIS MAN. I began this treatment on Monday morning.

Well, the following Monday morning I was sitting in the car waiting in front of a store where my sister had gone in to do some trading, when Mr.————— came up to the car and grasped my hand and said, "I'm sure glad to see you Miss—————. Won't you come up to the office and I'll pay you that bill?" So I went right along with him. When inside of his office he opened up his safe and took out a till and counted out the $60, just as I had done in my mental picture. Then he said, "I have just two more dollars in here and I am going to give them to you for waiting so long and not asking me for it." I thanked God for my money and that all was well.

Surely if you will put your trust in THE FATHER, and do your part there is no task too big or too hard to be accomplished. Trusting in God is one of the essential things to insure against failure, for with God there is no failure.

"MY GOD SHALL SUPPLY ALL YOUR NEEDS ACCORDING TO HIS RICHES IN GLORY BY CHRIST JESUS." Phil. 4:19.

CHAPTER VI

When Doubt And Fear Assail Us

OFTEN the beginner in Truth study finds himself facing many annoying, discouraging things and he stands still in doubt and fear, as I did many times in the beginning.

I came from a family that had a set creed, and I was taught from the tender age of three years that terrible things were in store for the ones that fell by the way-side.

So when I began to look around to see and hear of something more satisfying, it was quite a serious shock to my loving family. So when I began to demonstrate by New thought, they looked upon my activities in much the same way a mother hen does when her brood of ducklings (which she has had the misfortune to hatch) takes to the water rather than to dry land.

As a result of these conditions I had many many discouraging hours. Many of my well laid plans fell through because of my inharmonious environment. But by faithful, honest prayers and persistance, with faith in GOD, I won out and am now well and happy, for which *I give* THANKS TO THE LOVING FATHER. Many times when I was young in Truth I was tempted to cast it all aside and go back to my early teachings, especially when demonstrations were not exactly what I expected; but the wee, small voice would whisper encouragingly, "TRUST AND BELIEVE AND ALL THINGS ARE POSSIBLE."

Without faith you won't travel far. But with faith you travel straight ahead and with each step you gain a victory. With each succeeding victory comes PEACE, POWER, AND PLENTY. I used to think that I had more hardships and disappointments than anybody else and that I had more than my share of adversities. But it was not the case by any means. We receive just what we send out, be it good or otherwise. When you let your thoughts run unhampered on the negative side where hardships, disappointment, sickness and poverty dwell, you are sure to reap those things.

The next time your thought starts off on the wrong road, just make this statement and watch it retrace its steps:

20

I thank thee my divine Father, that I am one with thee: I am filled to overflowing with pure, peaceful thoughts, and the ever present spirit of faith, power and righteousness helps me to know all things and to love all things and to trust in thee. I thank thee that all is well and I am full of life, love, and laughter.

All things come through faith, but we must do our part by living right. Just what we put into this life is just what we get out of it. By sowing seeds of love and harmony we raise love and harmony, not sickness, or sorrow or strife. When we *live* the Golden Rule life will be a HEAVEN ON EARTH. Sickness, disappointment, and all inharmonious conditions will dissolve and fade away as if by magic and love, good will and fellowship will reign on earth. For all things work together for our good when we do the will of THE FATHER. If we lived right and had faith as big as a mustard seed, we could say to this thing, "GO", and to that thing, "COME" and they would obey. When we asked for a thing we would receive it at once. But we limit God's Power when we ask for a thing and think that a certain length of time must elapse before we receive. Just as long as we hold that attitude toward God's Power, we retard our achievement.

"I WILL GO BEFORE THEE, AND MAKE THE CROOKED PLACES STRAIGHT." Ruth 3:11.

CHAPTER VII

How A Love Suggestion Won A Husband For My Friend

I HAD known Alta many years and knew her to be a perfect daughter, and an all-around good girl, highly respected by all. But for some reason she wasn't popular with the young men. And there was one in particular who was very distant to her although she really loved him. Alta came to me one day and poured out her heartfelt, pent up feelings, saying, "I would make him a better wife than any one else in the world and I love him so much that I am sure in time I could win his love and

22

make him happy." I agreed with her and said, "You are right about it Alta. And we will tell him all about it too."

Then Alta exclaimed, "NO! NO! I couldn't do it and you must not do such a terrible thing."

But I insisted that we would tell him, but added that I meant to tell him in the silence. To this she readily agreed, so we set aside 15 minutes, four times a day, to tell Harry some very nice things.

First we repeated:

My heavenly Father, there is nothing in my life but love. I love everything and everybody, as thou lovest me. I love Harry————with all my heart and I ask thee, thou God of love, to bless the love mes- sage that I send to him and I thank thee that he does receive my love message and I have found favor in his sight.

We then repeated:

Harry————I, Alta———— love you and I do love to be your loving, charming and good wife. I want you to love me and make me a charming, lov-

able, good husband. I want
you right now.

We made this statement for three
days, then Alta called me on the telephone and informed me in a jovial voice,
"O Mizanna, Harry is to take me to
the social tomorrow night, and I am
so happy." And after three years of
married life they are still happy.

CHAPTER VIII

Another Case Where Sending Out Love
Messages Brought Love Back
To The Sender

RECENTLY a very attractive young
lady came to me for advice and
help. She was very much in love with
a certain young man, a bookeeper working in the same office with herself. She
told me of all his good qualities, and
how much she loved him and how hard
she tried to let him know without losing
her personal dignity. But it seemed as
if he was infatuated with another girl
that also worked in the office, and showed
his preference to a marked degree. This
situation had created hatred on the part

24

of my caller toward the other girl, and made her determined to win the fellow at almost any cost.

After she had told me all these things, and much more, she clinched her hands and squinted up her eyes in anger and said, "I *hate* her and I love him. I am determined not to allow anything nor anybody to step in between me and my desire. I will get him by foul means if I can't get him by fair ones."

I let her talk, and say anything she wished to say, for I knew it would do her good to get some of that pent up venom out of her system. After she had run down, and hadn't anything more to say, I had my turn. I had found out that the gentleman in question was a single man and that the other girl didn't seem to pay any attention to him, so I felt free in trying to help this girl. I said, "Well, my child, as long as you have such venomous thoughts I do not wonder that you do not get his love. That attitude would drive all love away. If you are going to try to *force* love to come to you, you do not need my help, for that isn't my way of working and trying to get love. When I want love,

I send out love messages, not *messages of hate.*" She then asked, "How can one send out love messages when there is so much hatred in life and heart?"

I again told her that to get love she must positively send out love. At that she began to sob, and as I also thought that a good tear flushing, would help relieve her soul of some more of the hatred, I just let her cry it out. But as she cried I treated her for love and peace and purity.

Presently she ceased to cry and said, "O, I know you are right and I really don't want to hurt the girl, but I do love H———— and I intend to have him, even if I have to make every one else unhappy to get him."

Again I shook my head, saying, "No, no, girlie, you are still wrong. You *positively must send out love messages, if you want my help, and if you are to get* the love you desire."

She then said, "Well, I will try your love messages and see if I can do any better." I told her I first wanted her to ask God's forgiveness, for all the hatred that was in her heart, and to ask for help to overcome the feeling. I then

told her to write this letter to H———
(but not to send it) and to read it over
the first thing in the morning and at
noon and the last thing at night, and
whenever she thought of him to say
something nice to him mentally.

The letter:

Dear H. . . ., we are the be-
loved children of God, the Father.
His love flows through us and
makes us pure, good and honor-
able in all our ways. I, Dona
C. . . . do love you with the pure,
good love that God gave me to give
to you and it is yours for the
asking. I thank God, the Father,
that you, H. . . . do love me
now. Your Loving Sweetheart,
Dona C. . . . . . .

I told her to read this letter for 10
days, then report to me. She did not
report in 10 days, but she came hurriedly
in on the morning of the twelfth day,
and grasped me in her arms and kissed
me, so excited she could hardly say,
"O, it has happened, it has happened!
H. . . . has taken me out three times,
and he has invited me to go with his

mother and sister, and himself on an outing. I did not know I could love everybody but I do and I am so happy."

CHAPTER IX

Being Healed, And Keeping Healed

IT IS a marvelous thing to receive the blessing of healing; but it is just as marvelous to be able to *keep* the healing, for many do err after being healed. Some people seem to think they can go on in the same old erroneous ways and still be free from all sickness, which is a rare thing indeed. For error, some time in life, is the cause of all the sickness that we have to contend with. To be able to keep healed one must live a life free from error. So we must be forever careful not to disobey any of the laws that come from God, the Father of Love. Of course, environment has a great deal to do with keeping one in tune with harmony and without harmony in your life it is a shallow existence, at the best.

Just as soon as you let go of God and one of God's laws, you will fall short of your all good; for we must be in *har-*

mony with the Divine at all times. So we should always be ready with a Truth statement and live within God's law of Love.

If I feel at any time that I have over taxed my strength, I lie down, arms folded by my side, and relax and repeat this:

My Father, I thank thee for thy wonderful love that is flowing freely through every atom of my being, purifying, strengthening, harmonizing and healing me. I thank thee for all the benefits I am now receiving. I am well and strong, pure of thought and act and I claim all that is mine, by divine right, and lo! I have it.

CHAPTER X

Praise As A Help In Keeping Healed

I REMEMBER early in life when I was quite inexperienced in Truth, that after I had been healed I was ashamed to say much about it. I feared criticism, both from my family and from my friends. So I kept my healing to myself, much as I would any other thing that I considered a private affair.

Well, I was fine at first. Then small ailments began to creep in and I began to doubt the healing, for I would reason with myself, if I was healed of all my diseases (and I had many) why did they come back? In the mean-while, my family and friends began to say I was failing, and amid all doubts and fears my old sickness came back on me in quite violent form. The family called the family physician and he in turn consulted two more physicians and a surgeon. After a half hour it was decided I was suffering from many ailments and should be taken to the hospital for an operation. The family stood tearfully by while I refused to be taken from home and asked that a friend of mine (a New Thought student) be sent for. She came and asked my family to let me stay until the afternoon, saying "If she isn't improved by then you can take her." My family consented to this and in one hour my pain was gone!

At this time my friend left me alone for a few minutes. As I lay quietly resting I heard my name spoken so plainly that I thought it was my friend—not my first name only, but my full name, and I answered, "Yes." Then the voice said, "GET UP AND READ THE 107th PSALM." For some reason I had the idea imbedded in my mind that there was only 100 Psalms, so I answered without turning my head to see from whence the voice had come, "There isn't any 107th Psalm." Well, in about one more minute the same voice spoke again, calling my name again just as it had done before, and I again answered the same way, that there was no 107th Psalm. All was still for a moment, then the voice spoke again, this time real loud, *"MIZANNA WOLFF, DO YOU HEAR?"* Now as the name "Mizanna" is of India origin and has a spiritual meaning and as it is a name that is very uncommon, (I have never known any other mortal to bear the name,) there was no mistaking that the message was for me. So I answered just as loud and emphatic, *"YES, I HEAR YOU, WHAT DO YOU WANT?"* for I did so wish to sleep. Then the message came clear and loud, *"GET UP AND READ THE 107th PSALM—NOW."*

I looked around the room to see who it was that insisted on my reading something that I was sure did not exist. Then I remembered that I was alone in the room and had been for the past 30 minutes. (The folks thought I was asleep and had staid out of the room.)

I then realized that the message was of Divine order, and I straightway looked for the 107th Psalm and found it. In that Psalm I discovered the *direct cause* for all of my sickness and sorrow, namely, I had been ashamed to claim my healing and PRAISE THE DIVINE HEALER FOR MAKING ME EVERY WHIT WHOLE. In that Psalm I was told where the trouble was, thus: "O that men would praise the Lord for his goodness and for his wonderful works to the children of men."

I am telling you truthfully that I began to PRAISE THE LORD FOR MY HEALING RIGHT THEN AND THE HEALING WAS SWIFT AND COMPLETE. I am still well and still praising the Lord for his kindness to his children.

"AND THE INHABITANT SHALL NOT SAY, I AM SICK. THE PEOPLE

THAT DWELL THEREIN SHALL BE FORGIVEN THEIR INIQUITY." Isaiah, 33:24.

CHAPTER XI

Peace In The Home

I KNOW a family of eight that lives in perfect peace now, yet a few years ago this same family was the terror of the neighborhood. They were also in a constant turmoil at home all the time.

Stories of an unfavorable nature preceded the entry of this family into our midst. At first they were very disagreeable. The mother and girls were unlady like and they were persistent gossips, even falsifying. The father and boys were always in trouble with themselves and with others. After they had gained the disrespect of the entire community, I decided it would be a Christian act to give them a peace treatment, so I used this statement on the whole family:

Dear Mr. and Mrs.————
and family: you are the beloved children of God and His love FLOWS freely through you, fil-

ling you with peace, purity, harmony and love. Everybody loves you and you love everybody and you are at peace with yourselves and with all the world.

In a surprisingly short time a great improvement took place in that family and at this writing (less than three years later) they are among the neighborhoods finest, best loved and most respected families. Peace reigns supreme in their home and affairs and peace also reigns in the neighborhood. When we reach the place in life where we can say we are at PEACE with all creation, we are then worthy of praise and we can ask for any just thing and we shall have it, even to raising the dead. And we will possess a joy that we would not exchange for all the pomp and glitter the world contains. So I always ask for PEACE and more PEACE, for it heals all wounds and leaves no scars.

"IF YE ASK ANYTHING IN MY NAME I WILL DO IT." John 14:14.

CHAPTER XII

How Fear and Deception Cause Nervous Ailments

FEAR and deception, I believe, are the cause of most nervous ailments. This may seem like a broad statement, but in my years of dealing with sick people, I have come to the conclusion that it is the truth in nine out of every ten cases that came under my personal observation, either fear or deception was the forerunner of the sickness that followed. I remember one case in particular that is foremost in my mind. I was called by a mother to come and treat her sixteen year old daughter, who was suffering with what seemed to be a bad case of nerves, (so the mother stated). When I arrived at the home the maid ushered me into the living room, where the mother was in great distress of mind, and she tearfully informed me that "Landa was very nervous," and asked me to please be very careful not to excite her as she feared for her sanity. Just then the air was rent with a scream. It came from upstairs and Landa said very plainly and positively: "I *won't* see her. Don't you dare let her come in here."

The mother begged me not to be offended at the poor dear, for "she doesn't realize what she is saying."

I entered the girl's room, approached her bed and smilingly said, "O, I beg your pardon, dear, but who is it that you do not care to see? I will tell the maid that you do not care to be disturbed."

She looked at me as I stood there smiling and she acted as if she couldn't believe her eyes or realize my presumption in coming in unannounced. She couldn't form any words, so she buried her face in the pillow and sobbed.

I stood very quiet and held the thought: "PEACE, BE STILL AND KNOW THAT I AM GOD." I stood so quiet that she thought I was gone and she soon ceased to cry and lifted her face out of her pillow and looked up into my still smiling face. A tiny smile played around the corners of her mouth, just for a moment only, then she began crying again. I closed the door, for I like to be alone with my patients, and sat

down, by her bed and took one of her
hands, remarking, "What a very pretty
little hand you have. You certainly
would make a wonderful musician or an
artist."

She smiled a wistful little smile and
said, "I can do both, but I like to paint
best."

I turned her hand over and said,
"Well little girl, you are wasting much
valuable time by allowing yourself to get
into the shape you are in to-day. God
gave you these pretty hands for you to
make use of, to be a blessing to others
as well as yourself, and you have no
right to let them lie idle. You cannot
do much in the shape you are now in.
Think what a pleasure you would be to
your parents if you were to win fame as
a great musician or an artist." All this
time I never let go of the PEACE statement. She lay watching me as if fasci-
nated. I said, "Now, little girl, I want
you to tell me what has happened to
cause my girl all this sad state of mind,"
adding, "you can tell me everything
and I will keep it just as you have told
it to me and I will do all I can to help
you, and to help you keep the secret that
is entrusted to me."

She replied, "Mother wants me to specialize in —————, and I just hate it and I don't have good grades in it and when mother finds it out it will be such a shock, for I have told her I was getting along all right. I couldn't bear to tell her the truth, for she does so want me to teach it. At first I tried to tell her, but she wouldn't take it seriously, she thought I was jesting. So I just quit trying to tell her and hoped that I might pass and everything would be all right. But it is just four weeks until examination, and I am so worried. I just can't bear to hurt mother by telling her I have deceived her, yet if I fail she will know it and there isn't any show for me to pass now."

Here she became hysterical again. During this second outburst, I caressed her hand repeating, PEACE, PEACE, ALL IS CALM. Soon she became quiet and I told her that we would hold a PEACE STATEMENT and see how quickly her troubles would vanish and how well she would get on with her work and surprise herself and still make mother happy by passing.

To this she consented, so we took the following statement.

38

I am now free from all fear, deception and hatred. I love everything and everybody and everything and everybody loves me. I am successful in all my undertakings. There is no failure for me, I am success. For I am a child of the all-wise Father. In Him is all my trust and I thank thee O God for my success.

Four days later I called to see her and after that she came to my home every day after school and we prayed and used the statement. She picked right up in her work. She told me the reason she didn't like the study was because she couldn't understand it, but with my help it was easy. Her teacher soon spoke of the great improvement in her work. When examination came she passed in all of her studies, to the delight of her parents and herself. And I was very happy too.

Last year this dear little girl taught ————— in the high school and she has the same position again for the coming school term. She is a child of the Truth now, and is a happy, healthy, good teacher. She scatters the **Truth** where ever she goes. The mother never knew the secret of her daughter's illness.

"FOR SIN SHALL NOT HAVE DOMINION OVER YOU." Rom. 6:14.

CHAPTER XIII

How A Friendship Of Years Was Strained To The Breaking Point, When Love Took The Helm And Steered Us Back To Harmony And Health

I RECALL one time in my life, when I was quite young in Truth, where not understanding how to deal with environment caused me a great deal of trouble. An old lady, a friend of the family for over 50 years, a girlhood friend of my grandmother, came to visit us without an invitation. The visit ran into weeks, then into months. In fact, nearly a year had elapsed and the prospect seemed favorable for a continuation of the situation. The lady was over 80 years old and she had not been able to use one arm for over 11 years. In addition to this she had not walked without the assistance of a cane for five years.

40

This made it necessary for me to help her to dress and to wait upon her a great deal, and give her time and attention that I really didn't have at my disposal. She was a constant fault-finder. Nothing was done to suit her. Everything and everybody was in the wrong. She had a set of rules for religion, and all other creeds were wrong, especially mine, she painted my future so very hot that Dante's Inferno left the cooling impression of a trip to the frozen north! The only thing I could see in favor of my future was the fact that I wouldn't have to purchase any warm clothing. No conversation was complete until she had expressed her opinion. She arrived on the scene early and she staid late. At last I began to feel as if I was losing my grip on the Truth and all that stood for HEALTH and HARMONY, and the ALL GOOD. This lady wasn't dependent upon any one. She owned a beautiful home and had a large income. And she was wanted at home, where her family gave her every comfort and care. But she liked to stay at our home, and she seemingly intended to continue doing so, despite the gentle hints that I much preferred otherwise. Many times I had endeavored to get her to accept my way of healing, explaining to her that all healing came from God. However, she scorned both me and my method of healing, remarking, "I have been trying doctors for the past 12 years and so far none of them have been able to help me and a few prayers won't be able to do what so many doctors have failed to do."

About this time I was very weary and worn. I had unconsciously developed indigestion and constipation and had a bad case of nerves. So in desperation I decided to treat both the lady and myself, thereby doing two good deeds at one time.

So the first thing in the morning and when she was taking her afternoon nap, and just the last thing at night, I would say silently, first speaking her name, then my own:

> We are perfect daughters of a perfect Father and His will in us wills us to be perfect and whole in every department of life. A perfect child cannot be sick, weak, or out of harmony with the father or with His crea-

tion. So we are well, we love
our home and our families, and
we do love to be at peace at
home with them.

I then thanked the Father that it was so
and that her leg and arm were healed
and that I was healed too.

After three days of this treatment my
friend said to me, "I feel so much better
the last few days, I have been sleeping
fine and I can get my arm up to my
head, I believe I can comb my hair now,
and I walked all around my room this
morning without my cane!"

I was so very happy I just had to tell
her the TRUTH, that I had been giving
her treatments and also myself, for our
complete recovery, and I added, "I am
all right now and I can see you are
too." Well this time, she took kindly
to my method of healing and promised
that she would hold the statement also.
And we praised God for our healing then
and there, after that, both of us would
sit together in the silence and hold the
statement.

I did not teach her the going home
part of the statement, but *I* held tight
to it for her. One morning, about a

week later, she came into the room without her cane! I was expecting this but when it came it really gave me a thrill. Also her hair was combed, something that she had not done before for 11 years.

We clasped our arms about each other and rejoiced and praised God, for we were both well and happy once more. One could hardly believe the wonderful change that took place in this old lady. Even her family could hardly realize what had taken place, when she went home to them well and so happy. For she did go home in a week after she was healed, and she was so useful and good in her home. This happened three years ago and she is still well, and she is planning on visiting at our home this summer and I am looking forward to it with pleasant anticipation. All the praise goes to the Father, the giver of all good gifts.

"CALL UNTO ME, AND I WILL ANSWER THEE, AND SHOW THEE GREAT AND MIGHTY THINGS, WHICH THOU KNOWEST NOT." Jer. 33:3.

CHAPTER XIV

How God's Law Of Love Healed
A Drug Addict

ONE evening I was called up on the telephone, and asked if I would come and stay for a few days with a lady friend of ours. When I arrived at the home I found our friend in great pain. They said she had suffered for three days without relief, only as the physician gave her an opiate and that the effect of the drug was spent in her and the physician was out of town and would not return until the next day. The lady's husband and mother were worn out waiting on her, trying to quiet her and ease her pain, so I told them to go to bed saying if she was not better in a little while I would let them know and we would get some other physician. What I really wanted was to be alone with her. After getting them out of the way I sat down by her and took her poor little hand in mine. (I have found if you touch your patient the help comes immediately) and said, "Now, Monta dear, if you'll try and stop that moaning just a moment and let me tell you something I'm sure you'll feel better." "O, I'm in so much pain," was all she could say. Then I told her that the body belonged to God and that it was her duty to help put it back into harmony. "But how can I?" she questioned. I told her we would first ask forgiveness for all misdeeds that we might have done, then we would send out a blessing to everything and to everybody, then we would ask for health and peace. My object in all this was to get her mind off her pain. (Usually I give a silent treatment, but in these things I always follow intuition.) This done I held on to her hands to keep them still and I never ceased for a second to hold to the *peace* thought. In just 30 minutes the girl was out of pain, and asleep. She slept for four hours with hardly a stir during that time. And all of this time I was giving thanks to the blessed Father for her complete recovery. Next morning the mother and husband could hardly believe their ears when we told them. But there was the proof before them. She ate her breakfast and went back to sleep, without the drug. She later confessed to me that she had been using drugs for over two years. The physician came the next day and spoke of how much better she looked. But when she told him what had wrought the change, he looked at me with a queer look, shrugged his shoulders and said, "O, it's all right if it's permanent but it isn't. She'll be wanting the drug again."

But I was determined that she should not want it, so I still affirmed the Truth statement. During the two weeks that I was there with her, we held the peace and harmony statement three times a day. When I finally went home the young lady was up and had not taken any drug during the whole time I was there with her. And she was free from pain so had no need for it. The best of it was she embraced the Truth and is now able to demonstrate the peace and harmony and all the good there is in life by keeping in tune with Divine Law and claiming peace of mind and body and power to cast out all that is not in full harmony with that Law.

"I HAVE HEARD THY PRAYER, I HAVE SEEN THY TEARS; BE-HOLD, I WILL HEAL THEE." 2 Kings 20:5.

CHAPTER XV

How God's Love Remade The Twins

WHEN I lived in Kansas City, one of our acquaintances was a father and a mother and two twin children, a boy and girl, 12 years of age. The father was a drunkard, and the mother wasn't much better. The children ran loose in the streets. The boy was a real rowdy and the girl was so uncultured that no one would tolerate her to play with their children. Every one saw so much bad in her that they couldn't see the good that was there. The neighbors all shunned the family and called them "the rough-neck family."

I was running a day nursery at the time and I needed an older child to help me with the 19 youngsters, so I asked the mother if she would let me have the girl for a while. The mother assented and also insisted that I take the boy too, saying, "You don't need to pay them anything. Just give them something to eat and they are yours if you can keep them."

Despite the protests of my family, I took these two children. You can hardly imagine the change that water and soap and clean clothing made in my little charges.

For the first three days I was almost sorry I had undertaken their care. I began to fear I had made a grave mistake. They were rude, careless with their language and in their personal appearance. They simply were void of any nicety. I was afraid they would never amount to anything and that I would have to let them go for fear they might make a bad impression on my other charges.

Then the thought came to me "Judge not lest ye be judged with the same judgment." I immediately asked God to forgive me for passing judgment on those children. I then began to use this statement on those kiddies:

Bobby and Betty, my sweet little friends, I love you and you love me and God loves us all. In the light of his love we are pure, sweet, good children, and we love to be nice to everything and everybody.

Whenever the children did something rude, I would tell them the proper way to act. When they said something rough or not just as it should be, I would reconstruct the sentence in the correct language. Then I would say, "Now children, that is the correct way to express yourselves, and it sounds so much better to use correct language." Now I am telling you truthfully, my readers, that the people couldn't understand how such a wonderful transformation could possibly take place in those two children, in three months time. When they spoke it was delightful to listen. ` They were mannerly, genteel and good and everybody loved them. And they actually made over both` their parents into new beings. The father quit drinking and their mother began to keep her home and herself tidy, and was a changed woman in every way. Despite the fact that their mother said not to pay them anything, I had paid them both regular wages and they were worth it too.

Betty was married last spring at the age of 18 and Bobby is studying to be an electrician. Both are highly respected and well liked by their associates. And all the praise goes to God the Father and I thank him for his love, for nothing short of God's Love could ever have worked the wonderful change in this family. This is just one example of what God's Love will do if we will only accept the wonderful benefits that are offered to all.

CHAPTER XVI

Praising Our Little Helpers Within For Best Results

WHEN my little boy and girl friends come to see me, I meet them with a smile and tell them how nice they look, and how very glad I am to see them. Then I drop all work for awhile and take them out around the grounds, and show them all of my pretty flowers and pick them a pretty bouquet, if it is flower time. And if it is fruit season I go to the orchard with them and get some luscious fruit for them. And if it should be between seasons that they come in, I take them out Kodaking, make them candy or do something to make them glad they came, and make them want to come back again. For they always bring me something nice.

51

Just so with our very own little atomic friends that dwell within. There are countless tiny atoms contained in our being to make it whole and perfect. Each one has its special work to perform. And whenever one of these tiny particles fails to do its work perfectly in every detail, there is set up discord in the body and we feel the results in a very short time.

Then as an act of appreciation to these little friends, upon whom our health and happiness depends, let us try praising them for their good and perfect work and thereby help them to express themselves in harmony.

I will give you my way of praising them. I have done this for over a year now and I feel fit at all times as a result. In the morning, on arising and as I take my bath, I say:

Attention, my entire being. You are the most beautiful, perfect and most lovable of all of God's wonderful creations. You are well, strong and capable. God's love is flowing through you, keeping you pure, good and clean. I thank God that you are perfect in all your ways, and that every atom is doing its perfect work.

Following are some special statements that may be used as desired or needed.

Treatment For The Face

As I give my face attention, I tell it how nice it is thus:

My skin, you are soft, clear and spotless. You are free from all undesirable conditions and you are glowing with radiant health and beauty. I thank God for this perfect condition.

Then, as I dress my hair I tell it how much I admire it with every stroke of the brush:

My beautiful, lustrous, healthy hair, you are fine, thick and elegant and I thank thee father for this wonderful hair thou hast given me.

For The Eyes

To my eyes I say:

You are so beautiful, strong and powerful that nothing is hidden from your perfect vision. You are clear, bright, fascinating and intelligent eyes. You see the all beautiful and seeing with good, perfect eyes makes all things look glorious and good.   I thank God for my blessed eyes.

For The Ears

I then say some nice things to my ears:

My most wonderful ears, you are not only good to look upon but you are perfect in hearing and understanding.   You are keen and quick to register all things good that you hear.   You hear with the ears of God and I thank Him for your goodness.

For The Mouth

To my mouth I say:

You are a pretty mouth.   Your corners lift in a most winsome smile.   Your lips are a beautiful rich red, portraying health and good nature.   You are a good mouth, for nothing unclean or defiled cometh thereout.   You speak for God and for the good of all, for which I thank thee, God.

If any part of my body does not feel absolutely fit, I give it a special treatment, just as I feel the need of, and as a result I keep well and happy at all times.

CHAPTER XVII

How I Removed 14 Lbs. of Surplus Weight In Three Weeks' Time

I HAVE told you in a previous chapter how I rebuilt my body from sickness and under weight to health and full weight. I will now tell you how I dealt with another problem.

I was most proud of myself for about a year, as I was almost the ideal weight. Then I noticed that I was not quite so trim in my clothes, and that I was becoming less active and graceful than formerly. The home folks and friends began to remark how broad I was getting. Not broad minded but broad of stature! So I consulted my old reliable mirror and sure enough, I *was* broad. Then I asked myself, "Why?" And the answer came back forthwith from the Spirit in me: "You set those flesh cells to work, didn't you?"

I answered, "Yes."

"And did you tell them to quit working when you had reached the desired weight?" said the Spirit.

"No," I admitted.

"You expect the milk man and the baker to leave you your milk and bread each day don't you?" asked the same questioner.

"Yes," I again admitted.

"If you told them to stop bringing their wares they would do so, wouldn't they?"

And again I said, "Yes."

"Well, just so with these flesh cells that you have bidden to work for you. When you tell them you want them to stop working, they will obey you. But you haven't told them, so they go right along doing as you told them to do. Now the thing for you to do is to tell them to stop working," informed the Spirit.

I then stood before the mirror and looked myself over. The sight was anything but pleasing. I weighed 154 lbs. whereas I used to weigh 105 lbs. As my height is about 5 feet 3 inches, either weight is an extreme. I felt that 140 lbs. would be a good balance, and I would still be plump. So I decided to check the action of building those flesh cells immediately. I called the cells to attention thus:

Attention, my entire being.
I am master of my mentality and
ruler of my thoughts and acts.
I say to this surplus flesh *go*.
(Here I touched my double chin.
Yes, it had gone that far). I
then placed my hands on all the
offending surplus flesh, and bade
each superfluous ounce to *go*.
Then I thanked God that it was
gone.

Every morning and evening I gave myself this treatment. At the end of three
weeks I was reduced to 140 lbs. I
thought that was near enough to the
desired weight, so I stopped my treatment.

I have had many more pleasant demonstrations, but this will serve to show you
what wonderful things one can accomplish by trusting in the All Good and
doing your part in life. I truly believe
one could raise the dead by asking God
to bless his efforts, and by living within
the God Law, realizing of course that
by yourself you can do nothing, but that,
"THE FATHER DWELLING WITH-
IN YOU, DOETH THE WORK." If
one would spend just a few minutes each

day in sweet communion with God, sickness, sorrow and poverty would be unheard of and Health, Peace and Prosperity would follow in its wake. Then we would realize what the meaning of THE KINGDOM OF HEAVEN AT HAND and we would be forever happy in this kingdom.

"COMMIT THY WAYS UNTO THE LORD, TRUST ALSO IN HIM AND HE SHALL BRING IT TO PASS." Psa. 37:5.

CHAPTER XVIII

The Transformation of May

ONE morning while I was in the missionary training school, a mother brought in a 12 year old girl "to see if I could make anything out of her."

May was a big strong girl, well matured, so I knew she must be a healthy girl. She seemed to be rather on the surly order and hard to get at, at least in her mother's presence. The mother said, "She refuses to attend school, she won't help me at home, and she won't work for anyone else. All she wants to do is to dress up and go visiting."

I made a note of all the mother's complaints, and told her to send May down the next morning as I wished to talk to the girl alone.

At nine o'clock the next morning May was announced. When she came into my presence she seemed ill at ease and bashful, so I said, "Well, Mayme girl, how is this good old world treating you this morning?"

She smiled a very sweet smile and said, "O Miss Wolff, I am so glad mama sent me to you, for I believe you will understand how I feel when mama scolds and threatens me. She doesn't understand that girls are different now to what they were when she was a girl; but I know you understand the difference." And I assured her that I did understand.

After I had questioned the child until I had found out all that I needed to aid me in helping her I said, "Now, May, your mother wants me to make something out of you and I want you to help me in the cutting, fitting and making, so that when you are finished you will be such a good, beautiful, charming creation that your mother will be proud of you and so surprised that it was possible for you to improve so greatly and so that *she will want us to make her over just like you.*"

At this May laughed out-right and said, "O my, wouldn't I be happy? I am so glad that mother brought me to you and I will do what you tell me to do *so there*. For you know how to say such nice things to one that you make them feel happy, and seem nice too. Mother never does say such nice things to me. She always scolds and threatens me and I don't like that."

I then told her that she must go to school and that she must help her mother all she could and that she must memorize a verse in the Bible every week and that she must come to see me three times a week, and repeat the following three times a day:

I am a perfect child of God, I love my home and mother.

God makes me good and keeps me well, my duties are no bother.

I love my school work and my art, because in life I play a part.

And I give thanks unto the Lord
that I am happy, well and
smart.

I put this statement in rhyme because
I have proven that children can memorize a rhyme much more easily than
prose.

In the meanwhile, I gave the mother
something to do also. I told her to
stop scolding and threatening May, but
rather to sympathize with her and take
an interest in what she liked and show
her the right way by comparing her with
some other girl that wasn't quite so nice
as she was and make her understand that
she was improving every day, every way.
I told her to affirm this often:

Father of love, wisdom and
mercy, I thank thee for my
beautiful, sweet, good girl and
that thy wonderful love fills me
to overflowing with love for
thee and May. I thank thee
for this peace and harmony
that fill my soul and for the
fulfillment of my desire and that
all is well.

May and I were much together that
summer, and she became a wonderfully

good, happy girl. This all happened six years ago and May is now a charming wife and an adorable mother herself. She is loved by all who know her.

And May's mother has also changed from the sick, fretful woman I first met to a happy, healthy woman who is a blessing to all whom she meets. *Thanks to thee, Father, always.*

CHAPTER XIX

How Visualizing A Trip to Florida Made It Possible For Me To Take It

I HAD always wanted to go to Florida, but I didn't see how I could spare the time or the money to go. However, the desire seemed to take possession of me to a powerful degree, so I began to make my plans to go. I first consulted a ticket agent who gave me much information and many booklets describing the more important points and giving the details to fare, accommodations, stopovers, important sight-seeing places, etc.

I next settled which route I would take and the places I wished to visit and where I could make my (visualized) money go the farthest and get the most pleasure out of it. I then planned about my luggage and wardrobe. I even made a list of the clothing I wished to buy and the price I felt I could afford to pay (for I didn't want to be wasteful.)

These things I visualized myself as buying, I saw myself packing my bags (for I had decided that I didn't want to be worried with a trunk) I even called a taxicab, for I was making this trip absolutely alone and I didn't intend that any one should be worried with the arrangements.

I also visualized myself as taking the trip after school was ended, so I could have at least three months all to myself.

It was January when I began to visualize and I took that trip every day in minute details until the first of May without one single thing materializing in my favor. Then things began to happen. First an aunt of mine came to visit us from the town in Florida that I intended to visit. I told her that I had planned to go to visit them, but I added, "Since you have come to visit us I won't go now." However in my mind I was taking that trip right then.

My aunt replied, "All the more reason

why you should go. You and the girls (meaning her daughters) would have the time of your lives. I have a round trip ticket and if you will go I will give it to you, and I will go to New York and spend the summer with Ella."

I could hardly believe my ears that I had heard aright, I was so very happy. So I thanked God for the ticket one way and asked him to help me to get enough money for my fare back. I now began to get ready in reality. I bought all the things I had planned to buy, and strange to say I bought them at the prices that I had visualized. So near in fact that on a bill of $52 I was ahead of the game 50 cts. Then my brother-in-law came over to our home one evening, and I told him how I was going to Florida and he said, "If you will sell my car for $800. I will give you $175. commission. Mr. G——— is in the market but I cannot deal with him." Again I thanked God for my victory.

The next morning I drove the car over and took the G——— family out driving and demonstrated the car, telling them all the good things I knew about it. I also affirmed all the time that they liked the car and that they would buy it. I left them at 10 o'clock that night. Mr. G—————— was to let me know if he would take it next morning. That night before I retired I asked God to help me sell the car and thanked him. And I went to sleep still affirming the sale and thanking God.

Next morning the telephone rang and I said, "That is Mr. G——————. He wants me to bring the car over." And sure enough it was him and he did want me to deliver the car! O, but I did praise God. When I delivered the car he gave me the check for $800 and I thanked God again.

I went to Florida, and had a most wonderful time. I made some wonderful friends and came home refreshed and enthused, ready for my fall work. I am still rejoicing in the wonderful kindness that God shows to the children of men.

"I WILL DO MARVELS."   Ex. 37:10

CHAPTER XX

My Personal Experiences With The Mind Telegraph

I HAVE often been asked, "Can one mind communicate with another mind," and I know that I am safe in saying yes, some minds can do so under certain conditions. I have had several positive proofs to that effect.

All my life, for instance, I would tell the home folks of things that were to happen or that had happened, when there was no possible way for me to know of these happenings except through communication from others' minds to mine. And several times in my life I have successfully sent out mental messages to others. Do not infer from this statement that I believe all can do this, for as to the truth of that I am unable to say. I speak only from my own experience. I could cite you to several personal experiences, but one or two will suffice I am sure to prove my point.

First, let me state that I have received messages as far ahead as six months in advance of the actual occurrence. At other times I have received the message at the exact time the incident happened, or a few minutes afterwards, or a few minutes before.

My first experience happened when I was about eight years old. I staid with my grandmother a great deal, and she was very strict about everyone always telling the truth in all things. So when I came in the house on this particular morning and told her that our neighbor Mr. X— was dead, she questioned me as to who told me. I could not tell her, for I did not know myself who told me or how I knew. Then followed one of the worst scoldings I ever got, she telling me where little girls went who told untruths, and how no one would believe me if I told stories.

While I was sitting ashamed of myself and in disgrace with my grandmother, Mr. X—s young son came into the yard after grandfather to come and help prepare his (the boy's) father for burial. When questioned as to what had happened, and when, the boy said that his father had a sudden heart attack and had passed out about 45 minutes before, just about the time I had received the message and had told my grandmother.

I was so badly hurt over my scolding that it was several years before I again ventured to tell the home folks anything, but I told others of things that would happen, and we would always find out that they had happened.

I have a very dear friend living at a distance and we send each other messages quite often. Not long ago I awakened in the night, startled by hearing my name spoken. I answered, "Yes." Then I heard my friend's voice say, "Come over at once. I need you." I looked at the clock and it was three o'clock in the morning. The first train left the depot at 5 A. M. So I began to get ready to go, for I knew she was in trouble. I arrived at her home at eight in the morning, and found her unconscious after an illness of three days. Along in the afternoon she regained consciousness and wasn't in the least surprised at seeing me. "I knew you would come to me when I sent you that message," she said. On inquiring as to when she had sent it, she said that "it was just as she felt herself failing, she guessed it was near morning."

I have another friend who lives over

3000 miles away and so we do not get to see each other very often. One day I was not able to get her out of my mind at all. Then a message came just as plain, in her voice, "I'll be in Kansas City at 9 P. M. for a two hour lay over. Please come to the depot."

Well, I went and sure enough there stood my friend waiting outside the door so we would be sure to meet. She expected me. She was going to her mother in the East who had been taken very ill. My friend had not known she was going until just a few minutes before leaving home. And she didn't know she was coming through my town until about two hours before. Having no time to telegraph me, she sent me a mind message and I received it. Now bear in mind that she would not have come through my town at all except for a wash-out on the road, and she had no idea of getting to see me when she left home.

TRUTH STATEMENTS THAT HEAL

WHEN making these Truth statements for healing, you can change the words to suit your own needs and thereby make the statements more personal to yourself. The main thing is to be sure that you never ask for a thing that isn't *in* HARMONY WITH THE DIVINE LAW OF LOVE. For whatsoever you send out, be it good or otherwise, it will come back to you. So, in view of this fact, one can see plainly that it behooves us to send out the good always. For by using good statements only, nothing but good can possibly come back to you. The object of the statements is to lift the mind *to the* CHRIST MIND WITHIN, WHERE ALL GOOD COMES FROM, AND ALL DESIRES ARE FULFILLED.

These statements can be used with equally good results, either for self-treatment or in treating anyone you desire to help. In treating another, just use his or her name in the statement instead of making it personal. *But if you should feel the URGE for a different statement by all means use it!* I receive a different statement for almost every case that comes to me. These statements are only to give the beginner an idea of how to apply TRUTH statements. The reader should be governed by his or her own INTUITION.

Prayer to Be Used Preceding Each Statement

I acknowledge thy presence, thou God of love, power and wisdom. Thou art everywhere present and in thy presence we have all that thou hast. We thank thee for the privilege of being in thy presence, where divine wisdom erases our hasty words and our mistakes, and where thy love grants us our every just want, and where thy power protects us from all harm. We thank thee, O Father, and ask thee to grant us our desire.

For Health

I thank thee, thou Perfect Father, giver of all good gifts, that thou art my life, my health and my happiness. In thy loving presence and power, I am perfect as thou art perfect in mind, soul and body. Thy love reigns supreme in all of my being and I am every whit whole. Health, strength and goodness fill my life.

For Success

I am a perfect child of my perfect father. I do unto others as my heavenly Father does unto me. I am just with all creation and all creation is just with me. I am one with prosperity and power. I

71

am successful in all my righteous undertakings. I give thee thanks, my gracious
Father.

For Love

I thank thee, God, that I am the child
of love. Therefore I am love. No hatred, fear or malice can mar my peaceful
existence, for God so loved the world
that He gave his son for us all. God's
love fills me with love for all. I am
happy in this love, for God is my love,
God is your love, and in God I am
happy, loving all and all loving me.

For Nervousness

My God of peace, love and harmony,
I know that thou art always near and
always willing to help thy children. All
I need do is to ask and receive. Therefore I cannot be nervous or fretful, for
thou art sweet calm, calm, calm. In
this knowledge I am made whole and
strong.

For Sadness

I am happy in thee, my God. No
sadness or sorrow can come into my
happy life, for in thy presence there is
only sunshine and gladness. I radiate
this sunshine and gladness. I am happy,
healthy and wealthy in this perfect state

with God, the giver of all good gifts. I thank thee for this happy, care-free life of gladness and sunshine; where all is contentment and bliss.

For Constipation

For best results one should have a regular time to attend to this natural function. Then use this statement: I thank thee my Father, that with thee there is no failure, and that every atom of my being is working to cleanse my body of impurities and dross, that the health and harmony which is mine by divine right is now released and has come to me. I am free, well and happy for no inharmony can come near me. I am thy perfect child. This statement cured me after I had suffered many years. I was healed of piles with the statement that follows, after the doctors said that nothing but an operation would cure me.

For Piles

I am created in the image and likeness of God, therefore I am perfect in every detail. All foreign matter dissolves and disappears where God's love reigns supreme. I thank God that I am whole, clean and perfect.

For Stomach

God mind in me makes me wise and discreet. I use good judgment in what I eat or drink. All my food agrees with me and gives me health, strength and pleasure. I thank God for the wholesome, pleasant condition he has given me. I do not worry or hurry. I use divine judgment.

For Liver Troubles

I love and trust every creature and every creature loves and trusts me, for we all belong to God. God's love fills my life with gladness. Where there is good will and gladness, no sickness or disorder can come. I thank thee, O Father, for perfect health, love and life. I thank thee that my liver is doing its perfect work now.

For Cold, Sore Throat and Grippe

My body is Spirit, therefore it is at its best always for Spirit is of God and all that belongs to God is good. I am free from all forms of sickness or distress. Only love, peace and wholeness dwells herein and God makes me free from all seeming pain. He satisfies and keeps me well, free and clean.

74

For Headache

I thank thee, O God, that thou art with me always. In thy loving care no pain, restlessness nor nausea can come. Thy loving care encircles me, healing, purifying and vitalizing every part. I am made whole *now*.

For Better Hearing

I do not look up or out for God, but within, and lo! there I find him. There I hear the wee small voice. I thank thee, O God, for the perfect hearing thou hast given me. I hear clearly all the good things thou wouldst have me hear. With this perfect hearing I am happy.

For The Eyes

This statement healed my eyes several years ago and they are still well. I first asked the Father to restore my perfect eyesight to me, I then claimed the promise in the following statement: I thank thee, my heavenly Father, the giver of all good gifts, that my prayer has been answered, and that I see plainly. I see with the eyes of my heavenly Father and my vision is perfect.

For Friends

I am thy child, O Father, and thy

loving kindness watches over me. I am divinely protected. No harm can come near me or mine. In thy loving care I fear no evil. I thank thee, O God, that love and good will encircle me. My life is full of friendship and friends. We are one with thee, in love.

For Business

I and the Father are one, and I am successful in all my just undertakings. I do unto others what is good and just and right, and as I would have them do unto me or mine, even as my Father would have me do whatsoever is honorable and fair, charitable and kind; that I do, and I give thanks to thee, O Father, for my success in life.

For Any Kind of Weakness

I am a perfect child of the living, loving, perfect Father. His love flows freely through me, cleansing, purifying and healing me. His love penetrates my every atom, vitalizing me through and through. My entire being is in harmony with the all good and I thank thee, my perfect Father, for my perfect health and strength. I am perfect in thy loving care.

For Any Kind of Distress or Sorrow

I, thy child, come to thee, thou God of love, for relief from this burden (state your case here). I ask thee to take it from me and free me from all discord and sorrow. I thank thee, O gracious Father, that before I have asked thou hast answered me. My life is full of love and liberty. I am free from every form of strife. Sweet contentment now takes its place for thou hast taken away my sorrow. I am at peace with myself and all the world.

For Strength

God is my life. God is my strength. God is my health. God is my good. God is my trust. God is my power. God is my love. God is my supply. In him I have all that really is, and it is good. I thank God for it all.

For Faithfulness

Sometimes one feels as if he had not been treated fairly; that someone has been unfaithful to him or to some trust. It is apt to have a very depressing effect on one. I have found that to feel that way about it makes us very hard in our judgment of others, and causes us to have a tendency to lose confidence in others, which is a very deplorable affair.

If I feel that I have been unjustly treated by someone betraying a trust, or not fully doing their duty by me or the trust that I have placed in them, I go into the silence. First, I ask God to forgive me for mistrusting this person or persons. I then ask for guidance and wisdom that I may be able to overcome the feeling; that I may be able to love and forgive them if they have treated me unjustly. I ask that I may be able to see only the good in them and try to be better and more true to my own trusts and friends. I then use the following statement:

I am now in the presence of God where all unfaithfulness, strife and injustice dissolves and fades away. Love, good will and sweet trust comes instead. I trust everybody and everybody trusts me. I give thanks to the divine Spirit for this true fellowship and friendship that I now have. I love and trust all creation and all creation loves and trusts me. I am faithful to all my obligations and trusts, and everyone is faithful and true to the trusts I place in them.

For Justice

If you would be treated justly at all times and under all conditions, you must deal justly with everybody and everything. When I say "everything", I mean every living creature, no matter how small or how lowly. You cannot treat one of God's creatures unjustly and expect to have justice dealt out to you. For whatsoever you send out is sure to come back to you. I have heard some people say when they were getting returns for their deeds, "O, I never did anything that I should have this come upon me".

Now, my friend, mistake not: You have or you would never receive what you are getting. I have seen parents allow their children to be so rough with their pets that it was positively cruel the way they treated the poor things. But when they or their children were in trouble they would feel terrible about it.

Here is the statement I use to establish justice: Thou art a just and a loving Father dealing justly with thy children at all times, I thank thee Father that I deal justly with my fellow creatures at all times. I thank thee, thou God of justness, that my fellow creatures deal justly with me at all times, that there shall be no evil happen to the just. I thank Thee for justice in my life.

For Prosperity

I am a spiritual magnet. I draw all good unto myself from my Father's storehouse. I draw perfect gifts and I thank thee, my heavenly Father, that all that thou hast is mine. My own will come to me for I know that thou givest the increase. I have abundance of treasures and gold. Prosperity dwells with me.

For Kindness

I thank thee, thou loving Father, for thy goodness and wonderful kindness to thy children. I thank thee because thou hast filled my heart with love, kindness and tender mercy for all creation, no matter how small or how lowly, for all creation belongs to thee. Therefore, I love all that is thine and all life loves me for thy sake, even as thou lovest all. I love all and show kindness to all.

For Peace and Power

In sweet communion with God, peace and power reigns supreme in my life and affairs. All discord dissolves into nothingness when brought into thy peaceful presence. I give thee thanks for this peace and power which is predominant in my life and affairs.

For Tender Feet

A man came to me one day so foot-sore and weary that he could scarcely stand. Since he was working as a collector for an instalment house he had much stair climbing to do, which not only made the feet sore and enlarged but had caused the arches to become weak and painful; also, his ankles were painful and badly swollen. He said he just couldn't lay off for a rest and wanted me to do something that would give him relief, if it were possible.

I told him to go home, remove his shoes, and massage his feet and ankles for at least 20 minutes, three times a day, holding this statement: Spirit is not subject to pain or disorder. I am Spirit, therefore my feet cannot be out of harmony with Spirit. You are strong, enduring feet; you are willing, capable feet. You delight in doing your work and you are perfectly able to do it. I thank God for my strong, good feet.

I didn't see my patient for a week for

I was out of town, but when he came to my home a few days later he came in walking briskly and free. Removing his shoes he displayed a pair of normal, painless feet. He told me that they felt better from the first treatment, saying, "I don't dread to climb the steps any more, thank God."

Miscellaneous Statement

There comes a time in most every life when we feel the need of a statement to make us feel stronger and more sure of ourselves. Here is one I like: In thee, O God, I put my trust and I thank thee that I fear no evil for nothing but good can come near me. I thank thee for this calm strength and endurance to accomplish all my just wants and needs, for the sweet peace that comes to those who wait upon thee. I thank thee, O God, that my desires are accomplished in the name of Jesus now, and that I am at perfect peace with all thy creation.

For Wisdom

God is a wise and generous Father. In his divine wisdom I know that I am wise with his wisdom. I have knowledge of all things and I claim my divine right

to health, wealth and freedom for which
I thank thee, O God.

For Purity

I am now in the presence of God where
all my just desires are fulfilled. I am
filled with purity, power and plenty. I
love to help everybody and everything
for I am filled with love for my fellow
creatures. I thank thee, O Father, for
this love and peace.

For Harmony

As mentioned before, it is very difficult to make a set of rules and expect the
mass of people to have the same good
results when they enter the silence, for
each individual will generally fall into
his or her own way of entering the
silence, but as a rule I sit for a few
minutes repeating, "Be still and know
that I am God". When that sweet
peace comes (which always comes when
one is at attention with God), I affirm:
My heavenly Father, I am at peace in
thy presence and I acknowledge thy
power and wisdom, thy loving care which
makes all things perfect and harmonious.
I thank thee for the perfect peace, harmony and wisdom that I now have.

For Life

I thank thee, thou living God, that I am free, fearless and vigorous. I love all life and have due respect for all life. Even the tiny little insects have a divine right to their lives and I thank thee, O God, for this love of life. All life is divine and belongs to thee.

An Affirmation For Each Day in the Week

Sunday

God's love fills me to overflowing, and I am at peace at all times.

Monday

God is my faith, my wisdom, and my liberty. In him is all my trust.

Tuesday

God is my peace, my prosperity and my power, and all is well with me.

Wednesday

God in me and I in him makes me fearless, free and friendly.

Thursday

God is my life, my love and my liberty and I am a child of God.

Friday

God is my health, my happiness and my harmony and I am made whole.

Saturday

God is my hope, my faith and my charity, and I am one with God.

* * * *

May God's richest blessing be with you who read this little booklet. May you be benefited by it, and may you prove for yourself that all that really is comes from God *and that it is good!*

The Author

The following mystical pictures are not related to this book.

They have been included for your enjoyment.

Pictures 1

Pictures 2

FAITH, HOPE, AND CHARITY.

Pictures 3

Pictures 4

Pictures 5

ALCHYMIA
(From Thurneysser's Quinta Essentia, 1570)

Pictures 7

Pictures 8

Pictures 9

Assyrian Type of Gilgamesh

Pictures 10

Pictures 11

MASONIC APRON PRESENTED TO GEN. WASHINGTON
BY MADAME LAFAYETTE.

THE GOLDEN WHEEL

Pictures 15

Pictures 16

Pictures 17

Pictures 18

Pictures 19

Pictures 20

CPSIA information can be obtained
at www.ICGtesting.com
Printed in the USA
BVHW061027250521
608096BV00011B/1857